Busted
What's Wrong with My Excuse?

By
Charles Patton

Busted, *What's Wrong With My Excuse?*
©Copyright 2024 Applied Market Solutions, LLC

Short Mystery Press
Book template by usedtotech.com
Cover by Book Design Company

Written for and owned by:
Applied Market Solutions, LLC
Contact: charlespattonbooks.com

_NOTICE

Throughout the writing process, I occasionally used chatGPT for tasks such as grammar editing, source identification, and content expansion/improvements. All of the core content is written by the author.

This book is a fundamental resource for professionals such as police officers, schoolteachers, and judges who regularly encounter myriad excuses in their daily interactions. It provides deep insights into the nature of deception and fallacies, empowering readers with the skills to distinguish truth from falsehood. Additionally, it equips them with practical strategies to address and counteract these excuses.

Let me share this quip from my wife in the spirit of this book. Reminiscing how flimsy the protective gear I used to play football in my youth was compared to today's gear, she said, "Just because you didn't know better doesn't mean you weren't stupid!"

Table of Contents

INTRODUCTION

This book is intended to be an entertaining anthology of the most absurd excuses—ranging from the pitiful to the preposterous—often concocted by criminals, politicians, and others caught in self-made sticky situations. We've all rolled our eyes at these tired justifications, but seeing them compiled in one place reveals a clear pattern:

Making up poor excuses often makes its practitioners laughable and unconvincing. Through a blend of humor and insight, this collection aims to shed light on the ridiculous lengths people go to avoid responsibility, highlighting the universal nature of this age-old tactic. By exploring these excuses, readers will better understand human behavior and the often-comical ways we try to navigate our own mistakes.

The Essence

Excuses are a sparkling dance of avoidance, where responsibility slips away, and fibs take the spotlight. They're not just simple denials; they involve crafting tales, shifting blame, or dressing up reality to escape consequences ranging from mild embarrassment to serious legal trouble. As the stakes climb, so does the inventiveness of the excuses—becoming more elaborate, fanciful, and sometimes even grounded in a sliver of truth to appear more convincing.

The Driving Forces

Driving forces behind excuse-making include safeguarding one's reputation or evading intimidating social, professional, or legal fallout. Additionally, the desire to avoid punishment, maintain personal relationships, and protect one's ego can drive individuals to fabricate excuses. For instance, a politician might fabricate a story to cover up a scandal, a student may invent an elaborate tale to explain a missed deadline, an employee might concoct an excuse to avoid reprimand for a mistake, or a friend might lie to avoid hurting someone's feelings.

Over time, individuals who frequently resort to fabrication hone their skills, becoming adept architects of fiction. However, for the astute observer, these constructed excuses often reveal their inherent weaknesses. Despite their complexity and occasional flair, a discerning listener can detect the contradictions and familiar patterns that indicate all is not as it seems. No matter how skillfully spun, the intricate web of lies often unravels under scrutiny, exposing the truth beneath the facade.

Underlying Strategies

Excuses often dance on a stage of strategic ambiguity, where obfuscation serves as the perfect shield against scrutiny. Cloak your explanation in a mist of vagueness, and the true motives remain concealed, just out of sight. A life lesson worth noting: presenting three plausible yet fabricated reasons can be surprisingly effective when queried about why something went awry. People tend to accept that three reasons sound reasonable, missing what's real.

Blame, too, plays a starring role in the art of excuse-making. It's a deft maneuver that shifts the spotlight away from one's actions. Point the finger at someone else, unforeseen circumstances, or external forces like the whims of the weather or the chaos of chance events. Blame creates a buffer, a safe distance from one's involvement, making it a favorite tool in the excuse-maker's kit.

Different Dimensions of Excuses

The relationship between lies and excuses is complex, extending on a continuum of deception and self-justification. Both involve an aversion to responsibility, but their dynamics differ significantly.

A lie is a deliberate falsehood shared with the intent to deceive. It seeks to create an alternate reality, allowing the liar to escape blame entirely. On the other hand, an excuse is a form of rationalization, often constructed to justify or mitigate one's or someone else's behavior. Instead of inventing a new reality, an excuse manipulates existing facts to lessen personal responsibility. While both tactics aim to avoid accountability, lies do so by obscuring the truth, whereas excuses seek to reinterpret it.

Scope: Big Lies vs. White Lies

Excuses come in various forms, ranging from blatant deceptions to what society commonly accepts as 'white lies.' Significant lies, often referred to as 'big lies', involve major ethical breaches, such as cheating or committing crimes like theft. Their revelation can lead to severe consequences, including loss of trust or legal repercussions. These big lies are akin to felonies in the realm of crime. On the other hand, 'white lies' are generally seen as minor and sometimes even socially acceptable deviations from the truth.

On the other hand, "white lies" are generally seen as minor and sometimes even socially acceptable deviations from the truth. For example, saying you're fine when you're not, just to avoid making someone else uncomfortable, is often considered harmless. These minor lies are more like misdemeanors in the context of crime.

The acceptability or impact of an excuse is significantly influenced by its deviation from the truth, the motives behind it, who it is meant to protect (self or someone else), and how the recipient perceives it. A minor lie to protect someone's feelings might be overlooked, while a significant deception intended to cover up serious wrongdoing is likely to be condemned.

The Role of Self-Deception

Self-deception occurs when individuals lie to themselves before lying to others, serving various psychological purposes, such as avoiding internal guilt or resolving cognitive dissonance. By fully adopting a fabricated story, individuals can present their excuse more convincingly because they genuinely believe it to be true. However, it's essential to recognize that this self-deception, while making the excuse appear more credible, does not alter its ethical or factual validity. It merely enables the individual to deliver the lie with greater conviction.

The Role of Conviction

Conviction in one's excuses differs from self-deception. Conviction, which is the strength and sincerity with which someone delivers an excuse, plays a crucial role in its acceptance, regardless of its truthfulness. An excuse delivered with genuine belief and conviction, rooted in honesty, is often more likely to be accepted by others. This is because sincerity and detail can make it appear more plausible, reducing the social or material consequences if the excuse is believed.

For example, someone who genuinely experienced a delay due to traffic will convey that excuse with conviction and detail that makes it more believable, compared to someone who simply left their house late but tries to use traffic as an excuse. The former's conviction comes from a place of truth, making their explanation more convincing.

However, the lines between lies and excuses can blur easily. People may convince themselves that their excuses are valid explanations, thus engaging in self-deception. This self-deception obscures the distinction between a genuine excuse and a fabricated one, making it harder for anyone to discern the truth.

Detecting Lies: Insights from Judge Judy

Judge Judy Sheindlin, the renowned television jurist, shared her expertise on detecting lies in an interview with Fox News Digital. According to Sheindlin, a liar's body language and physical reactions can often reveal their deceit.

"First of all, when someone's lying to you, they're not going to look you straight in the eye. They'll try to deflect because the truth comes in the eyes," Sheindlin explained. She noted that women tend to get flushed around the chest area when lying, while men often start to sweat above their lips and on their foreheads, showing a bit of a glistening and may start looking from side-to-side.

But most importantly, Sheindlin emphasized, "if something doesn't make sense, it's usually not true. There are sometimes aberrations, but they are rare. Most of life has a rhythm. So if something doesn't make sense to you, it's usually not true."

One notable example from her show, "Judge Judy," in 2015, showcased her keen ability to detect lies. In this case, a young man incriminated himself and lost his case within 26 seconds. The plaintiff reported that her wallet was stolen, along with $50, gift cards, an earpiece, and a calculator. The defendant interrupted, saying, "There was no earpiece in there, ma'am." Sheindlin immediately recognized the slip, laughed, and quickly awarded the plaintiff $500.

SPECIFIC TYPES OF EXCUSES

Role of Details

The number and accuracy of details provided to support an excuse significantly affect its believability. Each detail must be credible for the excuse to be accepted. Notably, offering three supporting reasons often enhances the effectiveness of an excuse. This trio of justifications can create a more convincing and comprehensive narrative, increasing the likelihood that the excuse will be accepted.

Role of Intent

It's important to recognize that not all excuses are lies. Some are legitimate explanations for why something happened a certain way. The key factor that transforms an excuse into a lie is the intent behind it. If an individual knowingly provides a false explanation to evade accountability, the excuse becomes a lie. Conversely, if the excuse is based on truth, even if it is a weak justification for one's actions, it remains an excuse.

However, over time, the habit of making excuses can erode one's ability to distinguish between an honest justification and a lie, making self-accountability increasingly difficult. This blurring of lines can lead to a diminished sense of responsibility and a greater propensity for self-deception.

Cultural Differences

Understanding the varying perspectives on excuses and the avoidance of responsibility across different cultures, influenced by ethical or moral considerations, is crucial. Not all excuses are inherently negative; there are situations where making an excuse is understandable or acceptable. This understanding can foster empathy and respect for cultural diversity.

For example, punctuality is highly valued in American professional settings, where being late for a meeting is often considered disrespectful or unprofessional. In contrast, there is a more relaxed attitude towards time in many Latin American cultures, and arriving late may not be viewed as critical.

Similarly, maintaining harmony and avoiding confrontation are highly valued in Japanese culture. As a result, people may offer excuses to avoid causing embarrassment or conflict, which can be seen as a respectful and considerate approach. In contrast, in German culture, directness and punctuality are emphasized, and excuses for tardiness or mistakes are less tolerated, as they undermine efficiency and reliability.

Relevance

Excuses vary widely in their relevance and acceptability. Some excuses are inadequate attempts to justify behavior that could have been avoided or results that could have been prevented. These are not true explanations but admissions of significant mistakes caused by a lack of focus or gross irresponsibility. Such excuses often reflect profound personal failure, which might be forgiven but is unlikely to be forgotten.

For example, in 2010, BP executives made several excuses following the Deepwater Horizon oil spill. They cited mechanical failures and unexpected pressure surges as reasons for the disaster. However, investigations revealed that critical safety measures were neglected, and cost-cutting decisions were made, which could have prevented the spill. These excuses were widely seen as attempts to deflect blame for what was ultimately a preventable catastrophe, causing lasting damage to BP's reputation.

Consider the following types of excuses in response to the question, 'Why did you do it?' Regardless of the specifics, these excuses generally revolve around the theme of 'It's not my fault,' a common refrain that often serves as a shield against personal responsibility.

Excuses, whether minor or significant, often reflect underlying issues in decision-making and personal accountability. They highlight a reluctance to take responsibility and a tendency to deflect blame. This behavior is rooted in poor decision-making, leading to the need for excuses and perpetuating a cycle of irresponsibility and failure.

LACK OF CONTROL

In the realm of poor decision-making, excuses range from the blatantly absurd to the seemingly rational. This book compiles some of the most implausible excuses commonly employed by those eager to evade accountability. While these excuses might sound familiar, when assembled in one place, they reveal a glaring inability on the part of the excuse-makers to take responsibility for their actions.

At the heart of any excuse is a psychological refusal to accept responsibility. Whether to dodge significant repercussions, elude blame, or self-justify a questionable act, excuses serve as psychological shields against embarrassment or censure. Understanding this psychological aspect is crucial in dissecting the use of excuses in poor decision-making.

The first category of poor excuses is those claiming a "Lack of Control" over a situation. Classic examples include, "My dog ate my homework," or "I didn't mean to break your vase. It just slipped out of my hand." This line of reasoning spans many scenarios, from panic-driven decisions to impulsive actions in the heat of the moment. People might claim they were rushed, running late, or unable to think clearly, suggesting they were victims of circumstance rather than personal decision-making.

Moreover, the role of fear should not be underestimated. It often serves as a significant catalyst, urging individuals to act in ways they otherwise wouldn't and later resort to 'Lack of Control' defenses. This type of excuse is intended to allow the perpetrator to evade responsibility by ascribing their actions to external factors like time pressure or unforeseen distractions. Such excuses ultimately paint a picture of individuals unwilling to assume responsibility, opting instead to lay the blame on forces they claim are beyond their control. Fear, as a powerful influencer, plays a significant role in the poor decision-making process.

The following excuses reflect an aversion to accountability and reveal the critical flaws in the decision-making processes that lead to such justifications.

"Lack of Control" Examples

- **I panicked, lost my head**: Overwhelmed by emotion, bypassing rational thought.
- **I lost control**: Failure to manage my impulses.
- **I was in a hurry and running late**. Time pressure was affecting my decision-making.
- **I was afraid**: Fear was a catalyst for decisions.
- **I got carried away**: Influenced by heightened emotional states or external factors.
- **I got distracted**: External elements diverting focus.
- **I didn't want to do it**: Acting under coercion or reluctance.
- **The [devil] made me do it**: Shifting blame to supernatural forces.
- **God spoke to me**: Claiming divine justification.

BAD JUDGMENT

The realm of "Bad Judgment" excuses opens a box like Pandora's, one of the self-justification mechanisms, striving to attribute poor decisions to temporary circumstances, lapses in cognition, or momentary whims. Individuals create a buffer zone that protects their character from scrutiny by shifting blame away from their core selves. However, this approach often overlooks the intricate tapestry of emotional, psychological, and social factors that make these lapses in judgment possible and sometimes even likely. By failing to address the deeper issues at play, these excuses only perpetuate a cycle of poor decision-making and evasion of proper accountability.

Emotional Triggers and Bad Judgment

One element often unexplored in "Bad Judgment" excuses is the role of emotional states. Phrases like "I was upset," "I was sleep-deprived, so I didn't know what I was doing," or "I was jealous" are frequently invoked to explain poor decisions, subtly suggesting that physical or emotional turbulence momentarily clouded rational thinking. While such states can impair judgment, using them merely as excuses after the fact misses an opportunity for self-reflection and growth. Instead of acknowledging these emotions as catalysts for poor decisions, individuals often use them to deflect responsibility, hindering their ability to learn from their mistakes and make better choices in the future.

Social Pressures and Groupthink

Sometimes, poor judgment occurs in a social context where groupthink or peer pressure plays a significant role. Excuses like "Everyone else was doing it" or "I didn't want to be the odd one out" fall into this category. The worst case is "mob psychology," as in the lynch mobs of the Old West.

In these instances, individuals divert responsibility to the group's collective behavior, conveniently ignoring their agency and ability to make independent decisions. This tendency to conform to group dynamics can lead to decisions that one might not have made in isolation, highlighting the challenge of maintaining personal accountability in social settings.

Long-term Consequences of Repeated "Bad Judgment"

It's also worth mentioning that a one-time lapse in judgment can be forgivable, but repeated offenses using the same excuse venture into character flaws. When "bad judgment" becomes a pattern rather than an exception, it raises legitimate questions about a person's integrity, maturity, and reliability. Persistent use of the same excuse indicates an unwillingness or inability to learn from past mistakes, suggesting deeper issues with personal responsibility and ethical behavior. Over time, this pattern erodes trust and respect, as others begin to see these repeated lapses not as isolated incidents but as a reflection of one's true character.

"Bad Judgment" Examples

- **"I was drunk (or high or off my medicines)."**: Lack of self-control induced by substances.
- **"I just thought..."**: Rationalization after poor foresight or understanding.
- **"I thought it was a harmless gag."**: Failure to predict the impact on others.
- **"It was just a white lie."**: Minimization of deceit.
- **"I just didn't tell everything."**: Omission as a form of deceit.
- **"I kept it to myself."**: Withholding information as a strategy.
- **"I was upset."**: Emotional states affecting judgment.
- **"Everyone else was doing it."**: Social conformity and groupthink.
- **"I didn't want to be left out."**: Social dependency.
- **"I didn't know."**: Claiming ignorance as a defense.

By dissecting the elements that constitute "Bad Judgment" excuses, we gain insights into the justifications people offer and the broader psychological and social dynamics influencing decision-making. These excuses shed light on the complexity of human behavior, revealing how individuals rationalize their actions. However, they often ignore the ethical dimensions, allowing individuals to sidestep moral considerations and avoid full responsibility. By examining these excuses critically, we can better understand the patterns leading to bad judgment and work toward fostering greater accountability and ethical awareness.

IGNORANCE

Another dimension of "Bad Judgment" excuses involves the claim of ignorance, often phrased as "I didn't know," such as "I didn't know it was wrong to do that. I thought it was just a prank." While genuine ignorance might exonerate some, there's a significant difference between not knowing and choosing not to know.

The latter, often called 'willful ignorance,' complicates the ethical standing of the excuse. Willful ignorance implies a deliberate avoidance of knowledge and responsibility, reflecting a conscious choice to remain uninformed. This type of excuse fails to justify the behavior and exposes a deeper level of irresponsibility and ethical negligence.

By claiming ignorance, individuals attempt to shield themselves from accountability. Yet, this claim often reveals a lack of integrity and a refusal to engage with the moral implications of their actions.

Excuses based on ignorance hinge on a purported lack of knowledge or awareness as the reason for poor decision-making. Phrases like "I didn't know what I was getting into" or "I didn't know it was wrong, illegal, or not allowed" suggest an absence of intent as if the individual stumbled into the situation unthinkingly. Similarly, statements such as "I didn't mean for this to happen," "I didn't realize that would hurt," or "I didn't know that could be dangerous" imply that the outcomes or consequences of their actions were unexpected or unintended, and thus, in the individual's view, less blameworthy.

While these excuses may seem less malicious than deliberate deceit or harm, they still serve to deflect responsibility. In many situations, claiming ignorance does not absolve one of accountability. Whether in a legal context, where ignorance of the law is generally not considered a valid defense or in a social setting, where basic norms are expected to be understood, these excuses often fail to withstand scrutiny. By relying on ignorance as a shield, individuals avoid taking full responsibility for their actions and sidestep the necessity for personal growth and learning. This evasion undermines trust and impedes the development of a mature and accountable character.

"Ignorance" Examples

- **"I didn't know what I was getting into...":** implies a lack of foresight regarding the scope or consequences of one's actions.
- **"I didn't know what I was doing...":** suggests incompetence or lack of skill invoked to avoid blame.
- **"I didn't know it was wrong, illegal, or not allowed.":** claiming unawareness of laws, rules, or ethical guidelines as an excuse; in court, "ignorance of the law" is no defense.
- **"I didn't mean for this to happen.":** indicates unintended consequences used to minimize culpability.
- **"I was only funnin'.":** trivializing one's actions by labeling them as playful or a joke.
- **"I didn't know that would happen.":** using surprise at the outcomes to divert blame or justify one's actions.

- **"I didn't know not to.":** invoking the absence of explicit prohibition to excuse actions.
- **"I didn't mean anything by it.":** attempting to downplay intent to lessen the perceived severity of one's actions.
- **"We didn't know anything else to do.":** presents a lack of alternatives to justify the chosen action.
- **"I didn't know he was going to...":** using the unanticipated actions of others to shift responsibility.

UNANTICIPATED RESULTS

Excuses based on "unanticipated results" are a variation of rationales that blame unexpected consequences to excuse poor decision-making. Similar to those based on "ignorance," these justifications often focus on the element of surprise as a shield against accountability. While they may sound superficially reasonable, such excuses often reveal more about the individual's limitations in planning or judgment than about the unpredictability of the situation.

Key phrases such as "I didn't expect..." or "I was shocked when I learned..." or "I didn't anticipate that the batteries in my alarm would die overnight!" are employed to present the excuse-maker as a passive victim of unforeseen events. For example, the excuse "I didn't think it would turn out that way" further illustrates this, implying that failure lies in the ability to predict the future rather than in making responsible choices in the present.

Ultimately, these kinds of excuses beg the question: where was the individual's due diligence? Responsibility partly lies in the ability to anticipate potential outcomes and act accordingly. These excuses generally don't clear the individual of blame; instead, they underscore lapses in their judgment or preparedness.

"Unanticipated Results" Examples

- **"It was a surprise to me.":** Trying to use shock as an alibi suggests an inability to foresee the outcome.
- **"I was shocked when I learned...":** Emotional surprise used to imply a lack of prior knowledge or ability to anticipate the event, suggesting that one wouldn't have taken the action if aware of the consequences. It often means that the individual wouldn't have acted if they had known they would be caught.
- **"Nobody told me...":** Citing a lack of external guidance or information as the reason for poor decision-making. This excuse may imply a failure of education or parental supervision, or that the individual was under the control of a leader and lacked personal responsibility.
- **"I didn't think it would turn out that way.":** Using failure to accurately predict consequences as a rationalization for the act.
- **"I failed my test because I got food poisoning (from eating old food that was in my refrigerator).":** One failure (in judgment) led to another failure (in performance).
- **"I didn't realize it would be this complicated.":** Claiming that the situation's complexity was unexpected and thus justifying the poor outcome.
- **"I assumed someone else was taking care of it.":** Using the assumption that responsibility

was delegated to others to excuse inaction or failure.

- **"I didn't know it would escalate this quickly.":** Suggesting that the speed of events was unforeseen, leading to a lack of appropriate response.
- **"I thought I had more time.":** Using a misjudgment of time constraints as a reason for not completing a task or making a mistake.
- **"I didn't foresee the side effects.":** Claiming that unexpected consequences of an action, such as side effects, were the reason for poor decision-making.
- **"I didn't anticipate that it would affect others.":** Using a lack of consideration for the broader impact of one's actions as an excuse.
- **"I thought it was just a minor issue.":** Downplaying the significance of the problem as a way to excuse not addressing it properly.
- **"I didn't expect to be held accountable.":** Suggesting that the lack of expected accountability led to poor decision-making.

DISMISSIVENESS

This category of excuses relies on minimizing the importance or intention behind poor decisions. When the reason isn't compelling, the individual often downplays the consequences. These excuses frequently come across as attempts to trivialize the impact or severity of the actions involved. While they may offer a superficial rationale for the behavior, they fail to acknowledge full personal accountability. The perpetrator is attempting to lessen the seriousness of their actions by minimizing or maligning the consequences. Comments like "I lost your keys, but it's not a big deal. I'll just pay to have them replaced" or "I crashed your car, but it's not a big deal. I have insurance" are attempts to downplay the significance of their actions by focusing on superficial solutions without recognizing the inconvenience placed on the affected person.

Such dismissive stances serve as roadblocks to self-reflection and growth. By neglecting to address the ethical or practical implications of their actions, individuals using these excuses evade immediate repercussions and avoid essential personal and social responsibilities. These excuses may backfire or be ineffective in a court of law if the consequences are, at face value, severe and deserving of punishment.

Dismissiveness Examples

- **"I was just joking.":** Attempts to recast the action as lighthearted, suggesting no harm was intended.
- **"I didn't mean to...":** Claims a lack of intent to absolve oneself from the consequences of the action.
- **"It was an accident.":** Portrays the action as unplanned to sidestep responsibility.
- **"They started it.":** This is a way of transferring the blame to someone else and attempting to absolve oneself from initiating the issue.
- **"It wasn't intentional.":** Emphasizes the lack of premeditation to minimize accountability.
- **"It wasn't my fault.":** Explicitly denies responsibility, often without acknowledging one's role in the action.
- **"It was an involuntary mistake.":** Implies that the action was beyond conscious control, thus avoiding culpability.
- **"I was misunderstood.":** Asserts that the adverse outcomes resulted from others' misinterpretation, not one's actions.
- **"I didn't really mean it.":** Reinforces the idea that the action lacks gravitas, suggesting it should be excused or overlooked.
- **"I said I was sorry.":** Uses an apology as a quick fix without addressing underlying issues, taking corrective action, or suffering the consequences.

- **"It was a minor issue.":** Downplays the significance of the action to avoid serious repercussions.
- **"Everyone else was doing it.":** Attempts to justify the behavior by pointing to the actions of others, minimizing personal responsibility.
- **"I was under a lot of stress.":** Uses personal circumstances to excuse behavior, suggesting that the situation justifies the action.
- **"No one got hurt.":** Highlights the lack of immediate harm to trivialize the potential seriousness of the action.
- **"It won't happen again.":** Promises future improvement to deflect current criticism without addressing the present accountability.

HAD NO MIND OF MY OWN

This category of excuses focuses on a perceived absence of personal agency to justify poor decision-making. When someone says, "I was following orders" or "I just did as I was told," they are essentially arguing that their actions were dictated by an external authority, absolving themselves of personal accountability. This tactic aims to deflect scrutiny away from the individual's role, placing the blame squarely on someone or something else.

Another set of excuses in this category, such as "I wasn't there at the time" or "I've never been there," goes a step further by seeking to remove the individual from the context of the action altogether. These excuses suggest that the person's absence from the scene is enough to clear them of any responsibility.

Additionally, other excuses like "I plain forgot," "I became enthralled by something," "I was late for work because I was sleepwalking and woke up in the park with no idea how I got there," or "I have an anxiety disorder" appeal to cognitive or emotional limitations as the reason behind the poor judgment. While these justifications may contain elements of truth, they generally fall short of addressing the person's integral role in the situation. By leveraging these excuses, individuals not only sidestep taking accountability for their actions but also undermine the broader ethical principles of personal agency and responsibility, attributing their lapses to forces beyond their control rather than acknowledging and addressing their shortcomings.

"Had No Mind of My Own" Examples

- **"I was following orders.":** Deferring to authority to evade personal responsibility, suggesting that the individual was merely executing someone else's directives.
- **"I was following my leader.":** Shifting blame to an external influence, implying that the leader's guidance absolves the individual of accountability.
- **"I just did as I was told.":** Forfeiture of personal agency in favor of obedience, indicating a lack of individual decision-making.
- **"I was following the lead of another.":** Laying blame on someone else's actions or guidance, suggesting that the individual was simply mirroring the behavior of others.
- **"I wasn't there at the time.":** Removing oneself from the context to sidestep accountability, claiming absence as a defense.
- **"I've never been there.":** Using absence as a form of denial, asserting that physical presence is necessary for culpability.
- **"I didn't see him.":** Claiming a lack of awareness to avoid responsibility, suggesting that ignorance of the situation absolves the individual.
- **"I plain forgot.":** Citing forgetfulness as an excuse for inaction or poor decision-making, implying memory failure justifies the lapse.
- **"I became enthralled by...":** Blaming external allure or distractions for one's lapse in

judgment, suggesting that fascination with something else diverted attention from responsibilities.

- **"I have an anxiety disorder.":** Using a medical or emotional condition as a shield against accountability, implying that the condition excuses the behavior.
- **"That's not who I am.":** Separating a single act from one's entire identity, particularly in instances such as sexual harassment or racial slurs. This excuse often follows an apology that may or may not be sincere and is sometimes combined with other excuses to create a multi-layered defense against taking full responsibility. One of the worst excuses because that "was who your were and may still be!"
- **"I was under a lot of stress.":** Justifying actions based on personal stress, suggesting that external pressures led to the behavior.
- **"Everyone else was doing it.":** Pointing to the actions of others to justify one's own, implying that conformity absolves personal accountability.
- **"I was just trying to help.":** Defending actions by claiming good intentions to mitigate responsibility, even if the outcome was negative.
- **"It was a momentary lapse.":** Suggesting that the behavior was an isolated incident and not reflective of one's usual conduct, minimizing the perceived severity.
- **"I didn't understand the consequences.":** Claiming ignorance of potential outcomes to

justify the behavior, implying that a lack of foresight excuses the action.

BLAMING SOCIETY

This excuse class seeks to shift the focus from personal responsibility to broader systemic or societal issues to justify poor behavior or choices. For example, when someone says, "I've had a hard life," they are attempting to frame their actions as the inevitable outcome of life circumstances they claim are beyond their control. Similarly, the excuse "I'm poor" aims to shift the blame onto societal structures that perpetuate poverty, implying that one's poor decisions are just symptoms of a more significant systemic issue rather than individual moral or ethical failings.

Comments like "I was late for work because of the traffic. It's so bad these days. It's like a war zone!" "I'm addicted to social media because of how it's designed. It's so addictive, it's hard to break away." or "I didn't get a good grade on my test because of the standardized testing system. It's so unfair; it doesn't measure my true intelligence!" attempt to externalize responsibility by highlighting external factors. Even a bully saying, "I got in a fight because of the bullying culture in our schools. It's so toxic, it's making kids' lives miserable," follows this pattern.

Another common rationalization in this category is "Everyone is doing it," which tries to normalize one's lapses in judgment by suggesting that such behavior is widespread and, therefore, somewhat acceptable. This logic employs collective misconduct to absolve oneself of personal responsibility as if the ubiquity of the action makes it somehow less objectionable.

More aggressive forms of this excuse class include statements like "If he didn't care enough to watch his goods, they were mine for the taking." This line of thinking embraces a sort of social Darwinism, a survival-of-the-fittest mentality where exploiting someone else's vulnerability is not only justifiable but even natural. It argues that others' weaknesses or carelessness legitimize one's unethical actions.

While some of these excuses may point to genuine societal issues that merit attention and discussion, they fall short as justifications for individual ethical lapses. Resorting to these kinds of excuses often serves as a smokescreen that clouds the core issue: the individual's accountability and moral integrity. Such rationalizations dodge the pressing need for personal responsibility, allowing individuals to sidestep the ethical ramifications of their actions while pointing fingers at society at large.

"Blaming Society" Examples

- **"I've had a hard life.":** Citing personal, but likely unrelated, hardships as an excuse for poor choices, implying that difficult circumstances justify unethical actions.
- **"I'm poor.":** Pointing to financial struggles as a justification for unethical behavior, suggesting that economic hardship excuses moral failings.
- **"Everyone is doing it.":** Using the prevalence of specific societal actions to normalize personal lapses, implying that widespread behavior makes the actions acceptable.
- **"If (the victim) didn't care enough to watch his goods, they were mine for the taking.":** Rationalizing theft or exploitation based on a flawed interpretation of social Darwinism, suggesting that carelessness in others legitimizes unethical actions, which conflicts with the principles of the rule of law.
- **"I was late for work because of the traffic. It's so bad these days; it's like a war zone!":** Blaming external circumstances for poor punctuality, deflecting personal responsibility.
- **"I'm addicted to social media because of how it's designed. It's so addictive, it's hard to break away.":** Pointing to the manipulative design of technology as an excuse for poor self-control and time management.
- **"I didn't get a good grade on my test because of the standardized testing system. It's so unfair; it doesn't measure**

my true intelligence!": Blaming systemic issues for personal academic performance, avoiding accountability for one's preparation.

- **"I got in a fight because of the bullying culture in our schools. It's so toxic, it's making kids' lives miserable.":** Justifying violent behavior by pointing to a broader negative environment rather than taking responsibility for one's actions.

- **"I couldn't pay my bills because the economy is in shambles.":** Blaming macroeconomic conditions for personal financial mismanagement or lack of foresight.

- **"I was just trying to fit in with my peers.":** Using peer pressure as a justification for unethical or irresponsible behavior, implying that conforming to social norms excuses personal lapses.

- **"The system is rigged against me, so why should I follow the rules?":** Rationalizing unethical behavior by asserting systemic injustice, suggesting that perceived unfairness justifies breaking the rules.

- **"I'm only human.":** Using human fallibility as a blanket excuse for poor decisions, implying that making mistakes absolves one of the needs to strive for better judgment and accountability.

- **"I didn't know any better because I wasn't taught differently.":** Shifting responsibility to upbringing or education to excuse unethical actions, suggesting that a lack of proper guidance justifies moral lapses.

DEFLECTION

The "Deflection" category of excuses focuses on redirecting scrutiny and responsibility elsewhere, often blaming external factors or specific circumstances that supposedly compromised one's better judgment. Phrases like "Someone else did it" or "It wasn't my idea" function to absolve oneself entirely as if to say, "I was a mere puppet in someone else's play." Similarly, the rationale "I wanted to fit in" leans on the crutch of social expectations, subtly shifting blame to collective behavior rather than owning up to one's actions.

The excuses "That comment was spoken when I was young" or "I was young and immature" provide a temporal defense, insinuating that one's younger self is a distinct entity, not to be held accountable in the present. The plea "I was under the influence" or "I was out of my mind" claims that an emotional or chemically altered state clouded one's judgment, temporarily turning off one's ethical compass.

While these excuses may add context, they usually fail to address the root issue of personal accountability and instead work to circumvent the vital processes of self-examination and moral growth. By deflecting responsibility, individuals avoid confronting the ethical implications of their actions and miss out on significant opportunities for meaningful personal development, thereby experiencing a loss in their journey toward moral growth.

"Deflection" Examples:

- **"Someone else did it.":** Shifting blame entirely to another party, thereby abdicating responsibility.
- **"I wanted to fit in.":** Citing social pressures as the driving force behind the action, subtly shifting blame away from oneself.
- **"It wasn't my idea.":** Claiming to be an unwitting participant minimizes one's agency and responsibility.
- **"That comment was spoken when I was young (e.g., racist comments).":** Arguing that one's past self should not be held accountable for actions or comments, implying that time has absolved the individual of past mistakes.
- **"I was young and immature.":** Utilizing age and purported immaturity as a shield from present-day accountability, suggesting that youth excuses poor behavior.
- **"I was under the influence of or out of my mind with (fill-in: blind rage, drugs/alcohol, grief, emotion, etc.)":** Invoking an altered state of mind as a defense, suggesting a temporary lapse in judgment rather than a character flaw.
- **"You shouldn't be getting on my case when you allow others to get away with x, y, z.":** Attempting to shift the attention from the perpetrator's actions to other unrelated activities that should get attention, thereby deflecting criticism.

- **"I was just following the crowd.":** Justifying behavior by claiming it was influenced by group dynamics, thus minimizing individual accountability.
- **"I didn't realize the impact.":** Claiming ignorance of the consequences to downplay the significance of one's actions.
- **"It was a joke.":** Dismissing harmful comments or actions as humor to avoid taking responsibility for their impact.
- **"I was provoked.":** Suggesting that another person's actions justified one's poor behavior, thereby shifting blame to the provocateur.
- **"Everyone makes mistakes.":** Generalizing the action to suggest that it is a standard human error, thereby minimizing its seriousness.

CLUELESS

The "Clueless" category of excuses capitalizes on an apparent lack of premeditation or awareness to avoid personal responsibility. Phrases such as "I don't know what made me do it" or "I just didn't think" paint a picture of haphazard impulsivity, suggesting that actions materialized out of a void devoid of meaningful intent. These excuses imply, "I was a ship without a rudder; my behavior moved by forces I couldn't comprehend."

Similarly, the excuses "It wasn't my fault" and "It surprised me" invoke an element of surprise or uncontrollability as if one were a mere spectator in their own life. Lastly, "I don't know what I was doing, but I'm here now" minimizes the action's significance by framing it as unimportant, disregarding its impact or seriousness.

While these excuses may appear less premeditated than others, they still act as avoidance mechanisms. Rather than confronting one's role in the unfolding situation, they focus on an alleged lack of awareness or intention, effectively sidestepping the essential processes of self-reflection and ethical maturation, thereby hindering personal growth.

"Clueless" Examples:

- **"I don't know what made me do it."** This common excuse Portrays oneself as a victim of inexplicable impulses, but it's a sign that deeper introspection is needed. "It wasn't my fault.": Shifting the blame to external circumstances or people, negating personal accountability.
- **"I just didn't think.":** Acknowledging a lack of foresight or consideration but avoiding more profound self-examination.
- **"It surprised me.":** Suggesting that one was merely a bystander to the event, caught off guard by its unfolding, and thus absolved from responsibility.
- **(Late to school) "I got locked inside my car.":** This one begs the question: How?
- **(Late to work) "My fish died, and I was too upset to come in.":** A touching sentiment, but a tad disproportionate.

HELPLESS

The "Helpless" category of excuses hinges on a narrative of personal impotence, casting the individual as a mere spectator in their own life, a puppet with its strings pulled by external or internal forces. Expressions like "I was driving too fast because I didn't want my fast food to get cold," "I had to find my cat," or "I just couldn't help myself" conjure an image of irresistible forces—whether these be emotional states, overwhelming circumstances, or irresistible temptations—against which the individual ostensibly had no defense. These phrases aim to elicit sympathy by portraying the person as a victim of circumstances beyond their control.

However, such justifications often backfire by inviting skepticism regarding the individual's capacity for self-discipline, ethical decision-making, and personal growth. An essential part of being a responsible adult is controlling one's impulses and making decisions that reflect ethical principles. When individuals resort to these excuses, they attempt to exonerate themselves and ignore the deeper issues: the need for self-awareness, self-control, and moral integrity. Essentially, they imply that a lack of situational or inherent control negates the necessity for personal accountability, which is an ethically and practically flawed perspective.

"Helpless" Examples:

- **"I couldn't resist it.":** Framing oneself as powerless against a particular temptation, thereby absolving oneself of the need for self-discipline.
- **"I couldn't do anything about it.":** Suggesting that one's circumstances were so overpowering that any form of agency was impossible, conveniently overlooking the responsibility to try to change those circumstances.
- **"I couldn't help myself.":** Invoking an internal or emotional state as a dominating force that left no room for reasoned action or ethical decision-making.
- **"I was overwhelmed.":** Portraying the situation as so emotionally or mentally taxing that any reasonable response was impossible.
- **"It was out of my hands.":** Asserting that the situation was beyond one's control, thus evading responsibility for the outcome.
- **"I was under too much pressure.":** Using stress or external demands as an excuse for failing to act appropriately or ethically.
- **"I had no choice.":** Claiming that circumstances left no viable alternatives, justifying the action taken.
- **"I was too tired.":** Blaming fatigue for poor decisions, implying that physical exhaustion excuses lapses in judgment.
- **"I didn't have the strength.":** Suggesting a lack of physical, mental, or emotional capability

to act differently, thereby avoiding accountability.

- **"I was too scared.":** Using fear as a justification for inaction or poor decisions, suggesting the emotion was overpowering.
- **"I was just following orders.":** Claiming that actions were dictated by an authority figure, thereby absolving oneself of personal responsibility.
- **"I was too emotional.":** Blaming heightened emotional states for actions, implying that they override rational decision-making.
- **"I was distracted.":** Using a lack of focus or attention as an excuse for failing to act responsibly.

PASSING THE BUCK

The "Passing the Buck" category of excuses operates on blame transference, contending that the onus for any dubious or harmful actions resides not with the individual in question but with someone else. Phrases such as "It's not my job," "I assumed you knew," or "The instructions weren't clear" present the individual as a passive participant or even a bystander, implying that they had little to no part in the situation and should, therefore, be spared any adverse consequences.

This approach neatly sidesteps the need to take personal accountability for decisions made or actions taken (or not taken), individually or as part of a collective. Another typical expression in this category is labeling someone else as "the troublemaker," which aims to direct the spotlight of scrutiny away from oneself and onto another party, serving as a diversionary tactic. For example, "I wasn't told about it" implies that the responsibility lies with those who failed to inform rather than with the individual.

This category, while potentially limited in its variety of excuses, unveils an interesting social mechanism: the designation of a scapegoat. By shifting blame in this manner, individuals not only distance themselves from their actions but also attempt to construct a buffer against further criticism, sanction, or accountability. It's a strategy that says, "Look over there, not here," when responsibility issues arise. However, such tactics often backfire by raising questions about the individual's willingness to take shared responsibility and cooperate with others, especially in settings where teamwork or collective action is required.

These tactics also impede personal development by allowing individuals to bypass the self-examination and ethical scrutiny necessary for growth and learning. In doing so, they undermine the crucial elements of personal accountability and shared responsibility, which are foundational to ethical conduct and social cohesion.

"Passing the Buck" Examples

- **"It's not my job.":** Deflecting responsibility by suggesting that the task lies outside one's designated duties.
- **"I assumed you knew.":** Shifting the burden of knowledge or communication onto someone else.
- **"The instructions weren't clear.":** Blaming inadequate guidance for one's failure to act appropriately.
- **"I wasn't told about it.":** Claiming ignorance due to lack of information, thereby avoiding responsibility.
- **"That was [someone else's] responsibility.":** Directly naming another person as the responsible party to deflect blame.
- **"I thought someone else was handling it.":** Implying that responsibility was delegated or assumed by another, thereby excusing oneself.
- **"It was [their] fault.":** Explicitly blaming another individual for the issue at hand.
- **"I was following their lead.":** Deflecting responsibility by asserting that one was merely following instructions or examples from another.
- **"I didn't get the memo.":** Using lack of communication as a reason for not taking action or responsibility.
- **"They didn't explain it to me.":** Blaming poor explanations or lack of information from others for one's shortcomings.
- **"I didn't handle that, my spouse (lawyer, accountant, or someone else) did.":** Aiming

to absolve oneself of responsibility by delegating it to another party, thereby avoiding any need for personal accountability.

- **"He or she was the troublemaker.":** Redirecting the focus and blame onto another individual to dodge personal scrutiny and responsibility while sidestepping the more complicated realities of shared accountability.
- **"They didn't get back to me in time.":** Blaming delays or lack of information on others.

TOUCHINESS

The "Touchiness" category of excuses revolves around the notion that someone else's actions or attitudes provoked an individual's poor or questionable decisions. Phrases like "He or she disrespected me" effectively characterize the individual as reactive, suggesting that their actions were practically obligatory in the face of perceived insults or slights. Similarly, excuses such as "I couldn't deal with him or her any other way" convey a sense of helplessness as if the individual had no alternative but to react poorly in the face of provocation. This excuse reframes their actions as being beyond their control, a reflex triggered by someone else's behavior.

More explicit rationales like "He or she deserved it" or "He or she was asking for it" elevate this dynamic to a form of self-appointed justice. These phrases suggest that the individual felt morally justified in taking matters into their own hands to deliver a form of 'deserved' punishment. This behavior aligns closely with a vigilante mentality, where the individual usurps the roles of judge, jury, and executioner, which clearly sidesteps established ethical norms and legal guidelines, underscoring the gravity of the issue.

The concept of "I was getting even - revenge" straightforwardly posits retribution as the core rationale, stripping away any pretense of responding to a situation in a considered and ethical manner. While these excuses may appeal to a sense of rough justice or resonate with individuals who feel they have been wronged, they nonetheless sidestep the moral requirement to deal with conflicts and disagreements in a socially acceptable and constructive way.

By anchoring one's behavior to the actions or provocations of others, these excuses divert attention away from the individual's agency and decision-making process. They undermine the importance of ethical conduct and introspection while offering an easy out from the rigors of personal responsibility and moral development.

"Touchiness" Examples

- **"He or she disrespected me.":** Suggesting that one's poor choices were a justified reaction to perceived disrespect, sidestepping any personal responsibility for the response.
- **"I couldn't deal with him or her any other way.":** Implies a lack of alternative options for managing the situation, thereby absolving oneself of the responsibility to act ethically.
- **"He or she deserved it.":** Frames the action as a form of self-delivered justice, ignoring the ethical implications and societal norms for conflict resolution.
- **"He or she asked for it.":** Extends the idea of self-justice by suggesting that the other party explicitly or implicitly invited the action upon themselves.
- **"I was getting even - revenge.":** Explicitly cites retaliation as the motive, negating the need for ethical evaluation or accountability for one's actions.
- **"I'm just having a bad day.":** Using external circumstances as a reason for a heightened emotional response.
- **"I didn't get enough sleep last night.":** Citing lack of rest as a reason for irritability, though it's a common fallback excuse.
- **"I'm under a lot of stress right now.":** While stress can make people more reactive, it's also used to justify touchy behavior.

- **"It's not you; it's me.":** A classic way to deflect blame and avoid conflict.
- **"You wouldn't understand.":** A way to shut down conversation and prevent further questions or criticisms.
- **"I've had a lot on my mind lately.":** Citing personal concerns as the reason for touchiness.
- **"I'm just a passionate person.":** Framing touchiness as a byproduct of one's intense feelings or convictions.
- **"I've been dealing with personal issues.":** Keeping the reason vague but pointing to personal troubles.
- **"I'm just tired of always being the one to...":** Defensiveness stemming from perceived repeated patterns or actions.
- **"I took it the wrong way; I'm sorry.":** An acknowledgment of overreacting, but also a subtle way to hint that the other person's delivery could've been better.
- **"It's just how I am.":** A resignation to one's nature, suggesting they can't or don't want to change.

SELF-FOCUSED

The "Self-focused" category of excuses reveals a distinct preoccupation with one's own needs, feelings, or ambitions, often to the detriment of others. This myopic focus manifests itself in various ways, from prioritizing personal desires over ethical considerations to disregarding the impact of one's actions on those around them. For instance, when someone says, "They wouldn't let me do what I wanted to do," they frame their desires as the most important factor, overlooking the potential harm or inconvenience their actions might cause others. Similarly, the excuse "I couldn't cope" deflects responsibility by foregrounding one's emotional state as an unquestionable justification for any ensuing behavior.

Phrases like "I was stressed out" or "I wanted the adrenaline rush" are particularly problematic because they prioritize the individual's emotional state or sensory cravings and imply that these feelings validate their actions, no matter how questionable. This belief can be seen as an abdication of moral responsibility.

Ambition-driven statements such as "I wanted to make a name for myself" or "I wanted to be accepted into the gang" expose a self-centered orientation that neglects the potential fallout for others. These are not just statements of desire but justifications for actions that may have far-reaching negative consequences. Excuses that stem from misunderstandings or perceived directives, like "I thought you said" or "But you told me," further exemplify this self-focused approach. These statements aim to shift blame onto others based on actual or imagined guidance, thereby deflecting personal responsibility.

More overtly, accusations such as "It's all your fault" or "You let ---- get away with it" actively redirect the blame, excusing one's actions by attributing them to another's supposed failures. As if saying, "I may have acted, but you caused me to do so."

Lastly, alarming phrases like "If I can't have you, nobody will!" take this self-focused mindset to an extreme, positioning one's desires as the sole factor worth considering, even if it means causing severe harm to others.

Overall, the "Self-focused" category is a cautionary tale about the dangers of egocentrism. While the feelings or ambitions cited may be honest, they are used to sidestep the more crucial issues of ethical responsibility, collective well-being, and moral growth. This class of excuses highlights the importance of transcending self-interest in favor of a more empathetic and ethically grounded approach to decision-making.

"Self-focused" Examples

- **"They wouldn't let me do what I wanted to do.":** Prioritizes personal desires over ethical considerations or societal norms.
- **"I couldn't cope.":** Focuses on one's own emotional state as the primary justification for poor decisions.
- **"I was stressed out.":** Cites personal stress as an all-encompassing rationale for questionable behavior.
- **"I wanted the adrenaline rush.":** Highlights sensory cravings or emotional highs as the main motivator behind actions that could negatively impact others.
- **"I wanted to make a name for myself" or "I wanted to be accepted into the gang.":** Reveals an ambition-driven, self-centered goal that disregards the potential negative effects on others.
- **"I thought you said..." or "I thought they said...":** Attempts to shift the blame onto others based on misunderstood or misinterpreted directives.
- **"But you told me..." or "Didn't you say...":** Implies that another person's guidance, whether real or imagined, is the cause of one's actions.
- **"I was following your lead.":** Suggests that someone else set the precedent for the action, thereby excusing oneself from individual responsibility.

- **"It's all your fault" or "You let __ get away with it.":** Directly blames another for one's own actions, as if they caused it.
- **"If I can't have you, nobody will!":** Takes the self-focused mindset to an extreme, implying that fulfilling one's own desires is more important than the well-being of others.
- **"I needed it more than they did.":** Justifies actions based on one's perceived needs.
- **"I was just taking care of myself.":** Uses self-care as an excuse for potentially selfish behavior.
- **"I deserve this.":** Belief that one's entitlement or deservingness justifies an action.
- **"It's what's best for me.":** Making decisions based solely on one's own well-being.
- **"I didn't feel like it.":** Prioritizing one's feelings or desires over commitments or responsibilities.
- **"I have to put myself first sometimes.":** A defense for decisions that may adversely affect others.
- **"It's just how I feel.":** Using emotions as a justification for actions or behaviors.
- **"I need to do what makes me happy.":** Using personal happiness as the primary guiding principle.
- **"I didn't think it was a big deal.":** Downplaying the significance of an action based on one's own perspective.
- **"I trusted my gut.":** Relying on personal intuition, even when it may lead to decisions others find questionable.

- **"I've been through a lot lately.":** Justifying actions based on personal trials, even if unrelated to the current situation.
- **"I'm just being honest about my feelings.":** Using candidness as an excuse for potentially hurtful remarks.

OUT OF MY HANDS

The "Out of My Hands" category of excuses purports that the individual was rendered powerless by external factors or circumstances, thereby avoiding personal accountability. When someone claims, "I was tired," or "I didn't have time," they're insinuating that their circumstances were so constraining that they had no other option. In this light, "I ran out of time" or "I was running late" serve as handy culprits for explaining poor choices or lapses in judgment.

Additionally, cognitive barriers are implicated in excuses like "I didn't understand," positioning lack of comprehension as a roadblock to proper action. The self-defense plea, "I was defending myself," cloaks the act under the guise of necessity and survival. When someone claims, "I owed them," it implies that societal or interpersonal debts somehow justify a predetermined course of action.

This category also features excuses that shift responsibility onto systems or structures, as seen in phrases like, "It was not my job" or "It was a design flaw." In these instances, the individual claims the fault lies elsewhere, be it the workplace, society, or even inanimate objects. The excuse "We didn't have the budget" further extends this reasoning by pointing to financial constraints as a compelling reason for inaction or poor choices.

On the lighter side, this category includes playful or exaggerated excuses like, "My dog ate my homework," which, while humorous, still seeks to shift blame to unpredictable or uncontrollable factors. The saying, "Not making a choice is making a choice," encapsulates the irony of this category: even inaction is a form of action, one for which the individual should take responsibility. Although these excuses might sometimes be grounded in reality, they offer a convenient way to sidestep the fundamental issue of personal responsibility.

"Out of My Hands" Examples:

- **"I was tired.":** Implies that fatigue rendered any other action impossible.
- **"I didn't have time" / "I ran out of time.":** Suggests an insurmountable barrier created by time constraints.
- **"I didn't understand.":** Suggests a lack of comprehension as the root cause for the action or inaction.
- **"I was running late" / "I arrived too late.":** Blames tardiness for a lack of better judgment or action.
- **"I was defending myself.":** Invokes the concept of self-preservation as the driving force behind the action.
- **"I owed them.":** Suggests that a literal or metaphorical debt justified the action.
- **"It was not my job.":** Attempts to divert responsibility to a system or another individual.
- **"It was a design flaw.":** Attempts to divert responsibility to a system or physical object.
- **"We didn't have the budget.":** Cites financial constraints as the limiting factor.
- **"My dog ate my homework.":** Humorously attempts to shift responsibility to an uncontrollable factor.
- **"Not making a choice is making a choice.":** Individuals should be held accountable for their inaction, whether conscious or unconscious.
- **"I did my part; the rest was up to them.":** Shifts responsibility to others.

- **"It's company policy.":** Defers to organizational rules to justify an action or inaction.
- **"The system wouldn't allow it.":** Blames technology or procedural constraints.
- **"I forwarded it to the appropriate department.":** Suggests that it was no longer their issue once it was handed off.
- **"The decision was made above my pay grade.":** Defers to higher-ups or superiors to avoid responsibility.
- **"I was waiting on approval.":** Indicates a dependency on someone else's action.
- **"It got lost in the mail.":** Cites uncontrollable external factors for the failure.
- **"I made the request, but they never got back to me.":** Places the onus on another person or team.
- **"The supplier/vendor messed up, not me.":** Shifts blame to external entities.
- **"It was the weather's fault.":** Blames natural occurrences for the issue.
- **"I was just following orders.":** Indicates that they were acting under instruction to avoid accountability.
- **"The guidelines weren't clear; the instructions weren't clear.":** Suggests that ambiguous instructions led to the situation.

EXTERNAL CAUSES

The "External Causes" category of excuses is marked by a tendency to absolve oneself of personal responsibility by pointing to external factors that seemingly forced one's hand. For example, physiological states like sleep deprivation or extreme hunger are frequently cited as conditions that hijack one's ability to make sound decisions, as in the excuses "I was sleep-deprived" or "I was too hungry to think."

In more emotionally fraught situations, one may claim their actions were prompted by upsetting news or betrayal, as captured by the phrases "My spouse told me they are leaving me" or "My spouse cheated on me." In these instances, emotional upheaval is presented as an overwhelming force that precludes rational choice.

Similarly, the justification "I had something more important to do" evokes the idea of prioritization to avoid blame. This justification creates a moral hierarchy where the errant behavior is depicted as a necessary sacrifice, making it appear that one had no other option.

Some excuses aim to further distance the individual from the event by casting them in a passive role, as seen in statements like "I was there but had nothing to do with it" or "I was there but didn't know what was happening." These claims attempt to convert the person's involvement into mere luck, suggesting that they were merely caught in a situation not of their making.

Despite the genuine challenges external factors can pose, the essence of this class of excuses is the denial of personal agency. Invoking external circumstances as the driving force behind one's actions shifts the burden of moral responsibility away from oneself. Such justifications may describe authentic difficulties, but they fall short of acknowledging that even in the face of external pressures, ethical decisions are still within one's purview. By relying on these excuses, individuals avoid the crucial work of introspection and moral growth, instead placing the blame on external conditions or other people.

"External Causes" Examples

- **"I was sleep-deprived.":** Citing lack of sleep as a reason for poor decision-making. While sleep deprivation can affect cognition, it often sidesteps accountability for poor choices.
- **"I was too hungry to think.":** Using hunger as an excuse for lapses in judgment. This excuse omits the individual's responsibility to manage their physiological needs and act responsibly.
- **"My spouse told me they are leaving me.":** Claiming emotional distress from personal relationships as a justification for actions, suggesting that one's emotional state absolves them of their responsibilities.
- **"My spouse (or other lover/special friend) cheated on me.":** Using betrayal to explain and excuse one's behavior while failing to address the individual's responsibility to manage their reactions constructively.
- **"I had something more important to do.":** Prioritizing other tasks to avoid taking responsibility for the action in question. Life often presents competing priorities, but individuals are still responsible for managing their time and commitments effectively.
- **"I was there but had nothing to do with it.":** Asserting presence without participation to deny responsibility, implying that one's mere presence did not impact the outcome.
- **"I was there but didn't know what was happening.":** Claiming ignorance of the situation to distance oneself from responsibility,

avoiding accountability for not being more informed or proactive.

- **"It was not my job.":** Attempts to divert responsibility to a system or another individual.
- **"It was a design flaw.":** Attempts to divert responsibility to a system or physical object.
- **"We didn't have the budget.":** Cites financial constraints as the limiting factor.
- **"My dog ate my homework.":** Humorously attempts to shift responsibility to an uncontrollable factor.
- **"Not making a choice is making a choice.":** Individuals should be held accountable for their inaction, whether conscious or unconscious.
- **"I did my part; the rest was up to them.":** Shifts responsibility to others.
- **"It's company policy.":** Defers to organizational rules to justify an action or inaction.
- **"The system wouldn't allow it.":** Blames technology or procedural constraints.
- **"I forwarded it to the appropriate department.":** Suggests that it was no longer their issue once it was handed off.
- **"The decision was made above my pay grade.":** Defers to higher-ups or superiors to avoid responsibility.
- **"I was waiting on approval.":** Indicates a dependency on someone else's action.
- **"It got lost in the mail.":** Cites uncontrollable external factors for the failure.

- **"I made the request, but they never got back to me.":** Places the onus on another person or team.
- **"The supplier/vendor messed up, not me.":** Shifts blame to external entities.
- **"It was the weather's fault.":** Blames natural occurrences for the issue.
- **"I was just following orders.":** Indicates that they were acting under instruction to avoid accountability.
- **"The guidelines weren't clear; the Instructions weren't clear.":** Suggests that ambiguous instructions led to the situation.

STINKIN' THINKIN'

Indeed, the "Stinkin' Thinkin'" category of excuses illuminates the complex interplay between flawed reasoning, ethical disengagement, and a lack of self-awareness. Excuses that start with "But I thought..." or "I just thought" often act as the preamble to justifications based on subjective assumptions, misunderstandings, or even willful ignorance. For example, one might hear statements like, "But I thought it would be fine if I didn't turn in the assignment on time because I'm generally a good student," or "I just thought it was okay to share her secret because she's usually open about things."

These excuses are particularly concerning because they are inherently self-referential, placing the individual's perspective above objective facts or universally accepted ethical standards. It's as if thinking something—no matter how poorly reasoned—grants license for the action to occur. It also suggests a lack of due diligence in confirming these assumptions with reality or considering the perspectives of others involved.

"Stinkin' Thinkin'" is a term commonly associated with the mindset often found in alcoholics, characterized by negative, self-defeating thought patterns that perpetuate the cycle of addiction. This type of thinking involves rationalizing harmful behaviors, blaming others for personal problems, and maintaining a pessimistic outlook. It hinders recovery by preventing individuals from taking responsibility for their actions and recognizing the need for change. Addressing "Stinkin' Thinkin'" is crucial in addiction recovery programs, as transforming these destructive thought patterns into positive, constructive ones is essential for achieving lasting sobriety and personal growth.

Moreover, these excuses can indicate more profound issues, such as a sense of entitlement to act based on personal whims, impulsivity that overrides careful consideration, or a casual disregard for other people's boundaries, expectations, or feelings. By attributing the action to a thought—regardless of its validity—the person using the excuse absolves themselves of the need for further reflection or apology. Such excuses are often prevalent among those who frequently abuse alcohol, as alcoholics are known for relying on this type of reasoning.

The genuine hazard in this category lies not just in the poor judgment it often reveals but also in the reluctance to treat that poor judgment as a point for learning and growth. It's crucial to engage in self-reflection and critical examination of our actions. It enables intellectual and moral laziness where the individual is spared the difficult but essential work of critical self-examination and ethical development. By shifting the blame to a supposedly innocent thought process, these excuses pave the way for future indiscretions and ethical lapses, all while stunting the individual's moral and emotional growth.

Stinkin' Thinkin' Examples

- **"But I thought it would be fine if I didn't turn in the assignment on time because I'm generally a good student.":** Assuming past behavior justifies current lapses.
- **"I just thought it was okay to share her secret because she's usually open about things.":** Assuming permission based on past behavior without confirmation.
- **"But I thought everyone knew that already.":** Justifying sharing confidential information based on assumed common knowledge.
- **"I just thought it was a joke.":** Using humor as an excuse for offensive or hurtful comments.
- **"But I thought it wouldn't matter.":** Dismissing the potential impact of one's actions based on personal judgment.
- **"I just thought they wouldn't mind.":** Assuming consent or approval without actually seeking it.
- **"But I thought it was the right thing to do.":** Using personal judgment to override established rules or guidelines.
- **"I just thought I could handle it.":** Overestimating one's ability or readiness and using that as an excuse for failure.
- **"But I thought it was a good idea at the time.":** Justifying poor decisions by claiming they seemed reasonable initially.

- **"I just thought nobody would notice.":** Assuming one can get away with something because it won't be detected.
- **"But I thought it was okay to borrow your clothes without asking.":** Assuming that friendship negates the need for permission, ignoring the other person's boundaries.
- **"I just thought you wouldn't mind if I came over uninvited.":** Relying on past experiences and assumptions rather than consent, disregarding the other person's current situation or feelings.

BLAME THE VICTIM

Here's another attempt at expanding the "Blame the Victim" category of excuses, including the introductory paragraphs and examples:

The "Blame the Victim" category of excuses seeks to deflect responsibility for one's actions by pointing the finger at the person harmed by those actions. When someone says, "He was getting on my nerves," "He pissed me off," or "They made me mad," they're suggesting that their behavior is merely a reaction to some provocation. Emotional states like annoyance or anger are then used as a rationale for everything from minor discourtesies to far more severe misconduct.

This approach to excuses is deeply problematic because it effectively sidesteps personal accountability. Individuals dodge their ethical obligations by focusing on what the victim allegedly did wrong. The victim is thus doubly wronged, not only suffering the initial adverse action but also bearing the blame for it. This thinking fosters a toxic cycle where lousy behavior goes unchecked, accountability is lost, and ethical considerations fall by the wayside.

"Blame the Victim" Examples

- **"He was getting on my nerves**.": Implies that irritation caused by the victim justifies the respondent's poor behavior, making the victim responsible for the actions.
- **"He pissed me off."**: Places the blame on the victim, arguing that their actions were so infuriating that they left no choice but to respond poorly.
- **"They made me mad" / "I got angry" / "I get angry quickly."**: Shifts responsibility for one's actions onto someone else, suggesting that being prone to anger is uncontrollable.
- **"She was asking for it."**: Implies that the victim's behavior or appearance invited the harm they received.
- **"If they hadn't done that, I wouldn't have reacted this way."**: Shifts responsibility for one's reaction entirely onto the victim.
- **"He started it."**: Claims that the victim initiated the conflict, justifying the respondent's actions.
- **"She shouldn't have been there."**: Blames the victim's presence for the incident, implying they should have avoided the situation.
- **"They provoked me."**: Asserts that the victim's actions or words incited the respondent's reaction.
- **"He knew what he was getting into."**: Suggests that the victim was aware of the potential consequences and thus responsible for what happened.

- **"She made me do it. He made me do it; They made me do it.":** Claims that the victim's behavior compelled the respondent to act a certain way.
- **"They shouldn't have challenged me.":** Implies that the victim's resistance or confrontation justified the respondent's reaction.
- **"He was looking for trouble.":** Suggests that the victim's reputation or past behavior justifies the respondent's actions.
- **"She was trying to manipulate me.":** Uses perceived manipulation as an excuse for retaliatory behavior.

GOOD INTENTIONS GONE BAD

The "Good Intentions Gone Bad" category relies on the assumption that noble motivations are enough to excuse poor outcomes. When someone uses phrases like "I thought I was doing the right thing" or "I was just trying to help," they suggest their actions were driven by positive intent, even if the results were damaging or problematic. For example, "I thought he or she needed my help" or "I just wanted to help out" hint at an underlying altruism or sense of community responsibility. The phrase "I just wanted to talk" is often cited to suggest that the action had no malicious intent.

However, the 'Good Intentions Gone Bad' category is problematic for several reasons. It dismisses the necessity of informed, consensual involvement in the lives of others. Just because one believes their actions are 'right' or 'helpful' doesn't make them universally so. Furthermore, this type of excuse avoids responsibility for the unintended consequences of one's actions, regardless of their good intentions.

This category argues that good intentions should serve as a get-out-of-jail-free card, effectively sidelining the need for accountability and self-reflection. It fails to address that ethical responsibility extends beyond intent to the actual impact of one's actions. Good intentions can't replace good judgment.

"Good Intentions Gone Bad Examples

- **"I thought I was doing the right thing.":** Believing one was acting correctly to bypass responsibility for adverse outcomes.
- **"I was just trying to help.":** Reflects a belief that intentions alone justify actions, even when those actions result in harm.
- **"I thought he or she needed my help.":** Presumes to know what's best for someone else without necessarily consulting them, sidestepping informed consent.
- **"I just wanted to help.":** Broad claim of altruistic intent that ignores whether the help was needed, wanted, or practical.
- **"I just wanted to talk.":** Attempts to downplay the impact of an action, implying it was benign or well-intentioned, irrespective of how it was received.
- **"I was trying to make things better.":** Asserts that the intention to improve a situation excuses any resulting harm.
- **"I had their best interests at heart".":** Suggests that the motive of caring for someone should excuse any adverse effects of the actions taken.
- **"I wanted to fix the problem.":** Implies that the desire to solve an issue justifies mistakes or missteps.
- **"I was only looking out for them.":** Assumes that protective intentions are enough to excuse any adverse outcomes.*

- **"I thought it would be helpful.":** Suggests that the belief in the potential benefit of the action excuses any resulting harm.

*Do-gooder Syndrome: Colt Terry first characterized this behavior in his biography, "Colt Terry/Green Beret." It describes someone who causes problems by trying to insert their help when it isn't needed or wanted. This syndrome may also include compulsiveness in helping to the point of self-neglect or burnout, having unrealistic expectations, seeking validation or attention from their martyrdom, or acting out of guilt.

PSEUDO_SCIENTIFIC

Excuses in this category attempt to use the veneer of scientific reasoning or scientific language to justify specific actions or choices. Phrases like "There is no evidence that..." or "Lacking evidence to the contrary...." suggest that the decision-maker is acting rationally and data-driven. For instance, someone might say, "There is no evidence that driving without a seatbelt is dangerous," ignoring the body of research that suggests otherwise. Or they may argue, "Lacking evidence to the contrary, I assumed it was safe to proceed," overlooking the precautionary principle which advises exercising caution when definitive evidence is lacking.

The issues with this category are manifold. First, it often represents a misunderstanding or even a manipulation of scientific principles. It can also mislead by suggesting that decisions are based on rigorous scientific analysis when they are not. Moreover, it moves the responsibility for decision-making away from individual judgment and ethical considerations to supposedly objective external factors.

These pseudo-scientific excuses are a cover for a lack of critical thinking and a readiness to distort or misapply scientific data to suit one's agenda. They expose a dedication not to evidence-based reasoning but to manipulating evidence to serve one's ends.

"Pseudo-Scientific Excuses" Examples

- **There is no evidence that driving without a seatbelt is dangerous.":** Ignoring well-established research to justify risky behavior and oversimplifying complex issues into binary "evidence or no evidence" categories.
- **"Lacking evidence to the contrary, I assumed it was safe to proceed.":** Overlooking the precautionary principle and failing to exercise caution in the absence of definitive evidence, while shifting the focus away from personal responsibility.
- **"Science doesn't prove that my actions are harmful.":** Misusing scientific uncertainty to avoid taking responsibility for potentially harmful actions.
- **"No studies show that this practice is dangerous.":** Cherry-picking data or ignoring existing studies to justify continuing a harmful practice.
- **"Until science proves me wrong, I'll keep doing it.":** Using the lack of absolute proof as an excuse to avoid ethical considerations.
- **"There is no scientific consensus on this issue.":** Exploiting debates or gaps in scientific knowledge to justify questionable decisions.
- **"Without conclusive evidence, my choice is just as valid.":** Equating personal beliefs with scientific validity to sidestep responsibility.
- **"The research isn't settled, so I assumed it's fine.":** Ignoring the weight of existing

evidence to proceed with potentially harmful actions.

- **"I'm following the science that supports my view.":** Selectively using scientific findings that align with one's agenda while disregarding opposing evidence.

PARANOIA

The "Paranoia" category of excuses is rooted in a mindset that perceives external forces or entities as being malevolently focused on undermining or harming the individual making a claim. It capitalizes on phrases like "They are out to get me" or "It's a conspiracy to (...),'' creating a narrative where the individual is the embattled protagonist in a grand, often sinister plot aimed at disadvantaging them. This narrative serves as a convenient way to shift attention away from one's choices, actions, and ethical considerations, instead framing the individual as the unfortunate victim of nefarious forces they cannot control.

While it's important to note that some people expressing these kinds of sentiments might be experiencing real mental health challenges that warrant understanding and appropriate care, the "Paranoia" category often functions as a diversionary tactic. It redirects the focus from the matter at hand, constructing a protective smokescreen that makes it challenging to address actual issues or ethical dilemmas. In this way, the individual perpetuates a self-centered worldview where their actions, regardless of their impact on others, are always seen as justified responses to a threatening external environment.

The danger of this category lies not just in its evasion of current responsibility but also in its potential to eliminate any prospect for future self-improvement or ethical growth. By attributing all wrongdoing or poor choices to imagined or exaggerated external threats, the individual frees themselves from engaging in self-examination or moral reflection. They can continue acting without accountability, entrenching themselves in a cycle of irresponsible and possibly harmful behavior.

"Paranoia" Examples

- **"They are out to get me.":** Suggests that external forces are targeting the individual, justifying their actions as necessary self-defense.
- **"It's a conspiracy to sabotage/ruin/destroy me.":** Frames actions as responses to a perceived widespread plot against them.
- **"Everyone is against me.":** Uses perceived universal opposition as an excuse for behavior.
- **"They are sabotaging me.":** Claims that others deliberately undermine their efforts, deflecting responsibility for failures or poor choices.
- **"The system is rigged against me.":** Suggests systemic bias or unfairness to justify one's actions or inactions.
- **"They're trying to bring me down.":** Asserts that others are actively working to harm their reputation or success.
- **"Nobody wants me to succeed.":** Uses the belief that others are rooting for their failure as a rationale for their behavior.
- **"They have it in for me.":** Claims personal animosity from others to justify defensive or aggressive actions.
- **"I can't trust anyone.":** Uses a general mistrust of others as an excuse for not collaborating or following norms.

- **"They set me up.":** Suggests that others have orchestrated situations to ensure their failure, deflecting blame from oneself.

THE WORST EXCUSES

In exploring strategy and tactics, it's crucial to address the role of excuses—especially the worst ones. Poor excuses come in many degrees, but the most egregious often come from the most reprehensible actions and individuals. Let's delve into some of the worst and most dangerous excuses, their impact, and what they reveal about those who use them.

Dangerous Excuses

Dangerous excuses are justifications or rationalizations that not only fail to acknowledge the gravity of the wrong actions they attempt to defend but also pose significant risks to individuals, groups, or broader societal structures. These excuses can perpetuate harmful behaviors, undermine justice, and erode trust in institutions. They often involve deceit, deflection, or manipulation to shift blame and avoid accountability. Here are key characteristics of dangerous excuses:

- **Legitimizing Harmful Actions:** Dangerous excuses are often used to justify actions that cause significant harm to others, such as violence, discrimination, or exploitation. By providing a seemingly rational explanation, they can make these actions appear acceptable or justified.

- **Misleading Narratives:** These excuses often involve false or misleading narratives designed to manipulate public perception. By distorting facts, they can obscure the truth and prevent a clear understanding of the situation.

- **Eroding Accountability:** Dangerous excuses undermine the principle of accountability. By shifting blame or presenting a distorted justification, they allow individuals or groups to evade responsibility for their actions.

- **Instigating Conflict:** In some cases, dangerous excuses can incite further conflict or division. For example, using nationalistic or protective rhetoric to justify aggressive actions can escalate tensions and lead to broader conflicts.

- **Creating a Precedent:** When dangerous excuses are accepted or go unchallenged, they set a precedent for future behavior. This can normalize harmful actions and encourage others to adopt similar justifications for their own misconduct.

The Putin Doctrine: "Because I Can"

While Vladimir Putin has not explicitly said "Because I can!" to justify his invasion of Ukraine, his justifications echo this sentiment. He has offered several misleading and dangerous excuses, including:

- **Ukraine is not a real country:** Putin argues that Ukraine is part of Russia's "historical and spiritual space."

- **Ukraine is a threat to Russia:** He claims NATO is using Ukraine to threaten Russia, necessitating "demilitarization and denazification."

- **Ukraine is committing genocide against Russian speakers:** He alleges the Ukrainian government is committing genocide in eastern Ukraine.

These excuses have been widely criticized as false and misleading. Most countries do not recognize Russia's claims, and no evidence supports these accusations. Putin likely does not believe these excuses; instead, he justifies his actions to the Russian people and the world, possibly under the guise of "Making Russia Great Again."

Stinkin' Thinkin': Excuses provided to a Lenient Attorney General

Consider Alex Acosta, the former U.S. Attorney for the Southern District of Florida, who negotiated a controversial plea deal with Jeffrey Epstein in 2008. This deal allowed Epstein to plead guilty to state charges of soliciting prostitution from a minor, avoiding federal charges that could have resulted in a much longer prison sentence. As part of the plea deal, Epstein was sentenced to 18 months in prison, of which he served about 13 months, with the provision of spending 12 hours a day, six days a week, on work release.

Acosta's excuses included:

- **"He was a young man with his whole life ahead of him."**

- **"Boys will be boys."**

- **"He was from a good family."**

- **"He (or his father) has been a dedicated philanthropist."**

These statements reflect a deeply flawed mindset that prioritizes the perpetrator's potential and background over the victims' suffering and justice. Jeffery Epstein committed suicide after almost a month in custody pending Federal charges. At the time of his death, Epstein was facing federal charges of sex trafficking minors in Florida and New York. The evidence against him was substantial, and if convicted, he would have likely spent the rest of his life in prison. Where it not for the weak yet dangerous excuses above, a more stringent prison sentence in 2008 could have spared many young women from the trauma and exploitation they subsequently endured.

Here are other examples:

- **Brock Turner Case**: In 2016, former Stanford student Brock Turner received a lenient sentence for sexual assault, with the judge citing his youth and potential. This sparked outrage and discussions about how serious crimes are sometimes minimized with such excuses.

- **Justice Brett Kavanaugh** During his Supreme Court confirmation hearings in 2018, allegations of sexual misconduct from his high school years emerged. Some of his defenders implied that his actions were typical youthful behavior, though this was widely criticized as minimizing the seriousness of the allegations.

Deflection: Excuses to a New York Attorney General

Former President Donald Trump has frequently used deflection to criticize his legal troubles. In addressing New York Attorney General Letitia James's investigations into his business practices, Trump used a deflection excuse:

"While you are wasting your time charging me, you should focus on all the crime in your town."

On Truth Social, he labeled James "a terrible A.G. when it comes to protecting the people of New York State." By framing her actions as a distraction from more pressing issues, Trump attempts to undermine the legitimacy of the investigations, casting himself as a victim of political persecution.

James had been involved in high-profile investigations, including allegations of financial fraud and misleading asset valuations. Trump's rhetoric implied these efforts were politically motivated and misdirected. This deflection tactic is designed to shift the focus away from his alleged misconduct, rallying his supporters by portraying himself as unfairly targeted. Trump was subsequently found guilty of 34 felonies.

Here some other examples:3

- **Andrew Cuomo:** Facing multiple allegations of sexual harassment in 2021, the former Governor of New York often deflected by emphasizing his accomplishments and the political motivations of his accusers.

- **Bill Clinton:** During the Monica Lewinsky scandal, President Clinton often deflected attention by focusing on his work and political opponents' motives, attempting to shift the narrative away from his misconduct.

One of the Worst Excuses

One of the most common forms of bad excuses comes from attempting to dismiss past inappropriate behavior. A frequently heard excuse is: **"Those tweets were from when I was young, immature, and stupid."**5 This phrase is often used to justify past racist or sexually inappropriate comments. While people grow and change, using immaturity as a blanket excuse for serious offenses trivializes the harm caused and undermines genuine accountability.

Public figures often use this type of excuse to mitigate backlash for past offensive remarks or behavior, framing their actions as the result of youthful indiscretion. Here are some notable examples:3

- **Kevin Hart**: In 2018, comedian Kevin Hart stepped down from hosting the Oscars after old homophobic tweets resurfaced. He apologized and explained that the tweets were from years ago when he was still immature and had since grown and changed.

- **James Gunn**: The director of "Guardians of the Galaxy" was temporarily fired by Disney in 2018 after offensive tweets from a decade earlier surfaced. Gunn apologized, stating that he had been trying to be provocative and funny when he was younger, but had since matured.

The Broader Context of Bad Excuses

See other examples in the References. Bad excuses, whether used in politics, business, or personal life, create smokescreens that prevent genuine resolution of issues. They shift blame, avoid accountability, and hinder ethical growth. The worst excuses fail to address core problems, undermining the legal process and moral responsibility.

CONCLUSION

The worst excuses—whether stemming from questionable justifications for past behavior, dangerous rationalizations for harmful actions, or deflective tactics to avoid accountability—highlight the lengths individuals will go to avoid facing the consequences. These excuses exacerbate harm, perpetuate injustice, and enable future wrongdoing by absolving the individual of the need for self-examination or moral accountability.

Weak justifications might temporarily provide relief, but ultimately, they hinder self-improvement and damage credibility. Recognizing and rejecting these excuses is essential for personal, ethical, and societal growth. Only through genuine accountability can we foster improvement and justice.

Individuals should cultivate a mindset that emphasizes honesty, humility, and resilience to move beyond poor excuses. This obligation involves acknowledging one's shortcomings, taking ownership of mistakes, and learning from them. Doing so can develop a greater sense of integrity and build stronger relationships.

So, what is the course of action? Mature adults apologize, admit their mistakes, ask for forgiveness, and accept the consequences. This is the hallmark of genuine accountability.

INDEX

REFERENCES

1. chatGPT-4.2
2. https://www.cnn.com/2020/11/12/politics/depart ment-of-justice-alex-acosta-epstein/index.html
3. Examples of celebrities using excuses from the news:
   a. Kevin Hart: Kevin Hart stepped down from hosting the Oscars after old homophobic tweets came to light. This was widely reported by news outlets like CNN. He initially refused to apologize, saying he had addressed the issue several times before, but later issued an apology. Reference: https://www.cnn.com/2018/12/07/entertainme nt/kevin-hart-oscar-host-homophobic-tweets/index.html
   b. James Gunn: James Gunn was initially fired from directing "Guardians of the Galaxy Vol. 3" due to old tweets that were controversial. He was later rehired. Reference: https://www.bbc.com/news/world-us-canada-44884856
   c. Paula Deen: Paula Deen faced backlash for admitting to having used racial slurs in the past. Reference: https://www.theguardian.com/lifeandstyle/2013/jun/21/paula-deen-n-word-food-network.
   d. Kyle Larson: Larson was suspended from NASCAR for using a racial slur during a live-streamed virtual race. Reference: https://www.npr.org/2020/04/14/834274135/nascar-driver-kyle-larson-uses-racial-slur-during-virtual-race

e. Liam Neeson: The actor faced controversy for admitting to having violent thoughts about killing a black man years ago. Reference: https://www.bbc.com/news/entertainment-arts-47117177, heading: Liam Neeson: 'I walked the streets with a cosh, hoping I'd be approached by a "black bastard"'

f. Justin Trudeau: Trudeau, the Prime Minister of Canada, was photographed wearing "brownface" and "blackface" makeup in his younger days. Reference: BBC https://www.bbc.com/news/world-us-canada-49765224

4. https://www.cnbc.com/2022/09/22/donald-trump-lashes-out-after-ny-ag-letitia-james-files-fraud-lawsuit.html

5. Quote by Shane Dawson, a YouTube personality and filmmaker. He said it in a video apology in 2018, after resurfaced tweets of his containing racist, sexist, and homophobic remarks went viral. In the video, Dawson apologized for his past behavior and said that he was "young, immature, and stupid" at the time he wrote the tweets. Dawson's apology was met with mixed reactions. Some people accepted his apology, while others felt that it was not sincere. The controversy surrounding Dawson's tweets led to him losing sponsorship deals and being dropped from the YouTube Red original series "Scary Game Squad." Dawson has since said that he has grown and matured since he wrote the tweets, and that he is no longer the same person he was back then. He has also said that he is committed to using his platform to promote positive messages and to be a role model for his fans.

6. https://bard.google.com/ when asked if Putin used the excuse, "Because I can."
7. https://www.foxnews.com/media/judge-judy-shares-telltale-signs-someone-lying-like-courtroom

www.ingramcontent.com/pod-product-compliance
Lightning Source LLC
Chambersburg PA
CBHW061658120626
46550CB00003B/996